SCHOLASTIC

Grades 3–6

Fabulously Funny Idiom Plays

14 Reproducible Read-Aloud Plays That Boost Comprehension by Teaching Kids Dozens and Dozens of Must-Know Idioms

Marci Appelbaum & Jeff Catanese

Editor: Sarah Longhi
Content editor: Carol Ghiglieri
Interior design: Melinda Belter
Illustrator: Mike Moran

ISBN-13: 978-0-545-20457-6
ISBN-10: 0-545-20457-7

Copyright © 2010 by Marci Appelbaum and Jeff Catanese
All rights reserved. Published by Scholastic Inc.
Printed in the U.S.A.

7 8 9 10   40   16 15 14 13 12

New York • Toronto • London • Auckland • Sydney
Mexico City • New Delhi • Hong Kong • Buenos Aires

Teaching Resources

Table of Contents

Introduction

Time flies.

Hold your horses!

This is gonna be a piece of cake . . .

Idioms are everywhere in the English language—and they don't just serve to spice up our conversations or help us sound poetic. Idioms have become integrated in everyday speech across all walks of life. In fact, they're so pervasive, we often fail to notice them.

What makes idioms tricky for our students is that their literal meanings often have nothing to do with their idiomatic sense. What do cats and dogs have to do with a torrential downpour? Nothing, but when your friend tells you it's "raining cats and dogs," you know you'd better put on your galoshes. This discrepancy between the literal and idiomatic meanings is especially challenging for English language learners.

One of the best ways to teach idioms to your students is through exposure. The more idioms you can present to your students, the more idioms they'll learn and remember. *Fabulously Funny Idiom Plays* introduces students to 130 commonly used idioms, grouped by theme, in 14 humorous read-aloud scripts.

Experts have found that it is particularly effective to teach idioms in context. The plays in this book have been written with this in mind, to help nudge your students toward understanding. In addition, for each theme, we provide some background to prompt discussion and some after-reading activities to extend the learning.

Using the Plays in Your Classroom

One advantage of using plays to teach idioms is that by their very nature, plays require repeated reading and practice. As students rehearse their parts, they get repeated exposure to the text, which reinforces comprehension and learning. A second advantage is that, because plays are fun and compelling, students' engagement level is high.

Use these plays in as many different ways as make sense in your classroom:

- Whole-group guided reading

- Small groups and pairs

- Targeted small-group work for struggling readers and ELLs

- Independent reading

You can be sure that by reading the plays in this book, your students will get to know some of our most common idioms.

Other Helpful Ideas

HIGHLIGHT THE IDIOMS

Each play features at least seven theme-related idioms set in boldface type. For added emphasis, you might wish to use a marker to highlight the idioms so they really stand out in the text. Another idea is to provide students with markers and ask them to highlight the idioms themselves.

KEEP LISTS

Idioms are so ingrained in our speech and writing that much of learning to master them entails simple recognition. Ask your students to pay careful attention to their speech and that of their friends and family. Have them keep lists of anything they hear or say that they think might be an idiom. Then pick a time each week to discuss students' lists. In addition, keep a class list and add any idioms that you discover while studying other classroom subjects.

USE VISUAL AIDS

A fun way to help your students remember the meanings of some of the more confusing idioms is to draw them. Have your students fold a sheet of paper in half. On the left side write the idiom and the right side write the meaning of the idiom. On the left side have the kids illustrate the literal meaning of the phrase. On the right side of the page have them draw the figurative meaning. For example, for the idiom "in a pickle" students might draw themselves trapped in a pickle jar or dressed in a pickle suit to illustrate the literal meaning and a picture of a time when they were in a difficult situation for the figurative one.

CROSS YOUR CURRICULA

Use the idioms as starting points for lessons in other subjects. Many of the follow-up activities for each play will give you examples of how to do this. When studying idioms based on numbers, don't stop when language arts class ends—continue the lesson through math class, finding ways to connect a math lesson to the idioms you just studied. For idioms based on parts of the body, there is plenty of science to be had. This type of work really lets your students see how idioms operate in real-world scenarios.

Sports and Games Idioms

Idioms originating in the sports world are used widely in English, but apart from true sports fans, many of us—and most of our students—have never learned where these common phrases originated. Take the idioms "give it your best shot" and "par for the course." Did you know these terms come from archery and golf, respectively? In understanding these idioms, it certainly helps to know that a *shot* is an attempt at striking a target and that *par* means "average number of strokes to complete a hole."

Review the idioms in this chapter with your students and help them picture each one. After reading the play, use the follow-up activities to reinforce the meanings of the expressions, and encourage students to use the idioms in their own speech and writing. Your students may be surprised to see how many phrases they hear, read, and say every day come from their favorite sports!

Activities

1 Even though the idioms featured here originated in sports, they're used all the time in everyday conversation. Have each of your students pick five of the idioms from the play. Ask them to write a first-person narrative that includes all five idioms. Make sure they write about something *other than* sports!

2 Have your students look online or in books or listen to shows on TV to come up with their own list of five sports idioms that aren't used in this play. Ask them to include which sports the idioms come from, what the expressions mean in those sports, and how they are used in everyday language.

Idioms in this play

- blow by blow
- get the ball rolling
- racing against the clock
- strike out
- in the ballpark
- give a run for one's money
- no sweat
- par for the course
- put one through one's paces
- give it one's best shot
- out in left field
- win by a nose

Characters

Mr. Becker

Candace

Lynn

Jack

Oscar

Mr. Becker Gets the Ball Rolling

Mr. Becker enters the stage with a clipboard in his hand.

Mr. Becker: Okay, everybody. Gather around.

(Oscar, Lynn, Jack, and Candace enter with baseball mitts on.)

Mr. Becker: You all signed up for the baseball team, and since Coach Ramirez is sick today, I've been asked to fill in.

All: Yay!

Mr. Becker: Well, I don't know that much about the rules of baseball, so I'm going to need you guys to help me out.

Candace: Don't worry, Mr. Becker. We'll go over it all, **blow by blow.**

Mr. Becker: Blow by blow? Now hold on. There isn't going to be any fighting allowed while I'm the coach.

Lynn: Of course not. There's no fighting in baseball. Why would you think that?

Jack: Blow by blow just means step by step.

Mr. Becker: Oh, I see. I thought you were talking about boxing.

Oscar: Not at all, Mr. Becker. We just want to **get the ball rolling.**

(Mr. Becker looks at his clipboard.)

Mr. Becker: It says here that in baseball you throw the ball, not roll it.

Jack: You do throw it.

Oscar: Why would you roll a baseball? That's ridiculous!

Candace: We just want to get started.

Lynn: Mr. Becker, you'd better figure this out. The season starts in a week.

Mr. Becker: One week?

Candace: Yes! We're **racing against the clock!**

Mr. Becker: What clock?

Oscar: She means we have to be fast.

Lynn: Right. If we don't practice, we're going to **strike out!**

Mr. Becker: Ah! Strike out! Now that's something that I *know* is from baseball.

Lynn: But I mean the whole team will strike out.

Mr. Becker: Come on now, Lynn. I don't think the whole team will strike out. Someone is bound to get a hit.

Jack: You still don't get it, Mr. Becker. But at least you're **in the ballpark.**

(Mr. Becker looks around.)

Candace: Never mind.

Jack: All right. So what positions should we take?

Mr. Becker: Jack, you play first base.

Candace: But I want to play first base!

Jack: I'm better at first than you are.

Candace: We'll see. I'll **give you a run for your money.**

Mr. Becker: Jack, you play first base for half of practice and Candace can play for the second half. Okay?

Candace: Sure. **No sweat.**

Jack: That's fine with me, too.

Mr. Becker: Oscar, I need you in right field.

Oscar: But I hate right field. I never get the position I want, but that's **par for the course.**

Mr. Becker: Par for the course? That's not baseball, that's golf! Even I know that!

Oscar: I mean that things always seem to go that way for me.

Lynn: Where do I play, Mr. Becker? It doesn't matter to me.

Mr. Becker: Well, then. Why don't you pitch?

Lynn: Wow! That will **put me through my paces.**

Mr. Becker: No, Lynn. That's the position where you throw the ball.

Lynn: I know that, Mr. Becker. I just mean that it will be a tough position to play.

Mr. Becker: Oh, right. But you can do it.

Lynn: I'll **give it my best shot.**

Oscar: What about Bobby? He's coming, but he said he can't play until he finds his lucky cap.

Jack: That's *so* Bobby! He's always a little **out in left field.**

Mr. Becker: Left field? I was going to have him as shortstop.

Jack: Mr. Becker! I mean he's a little eccentric!

Candace: Gee, Mr. Becker. For a teacher, you sure don't know a lot about what's going on.

Mr. Becker: Gee, Candace. For a student, you sure don't know a lot about getting your homework done on time.

Jack: Oh! Mr. Becker **wins by a nose!**

Mr. Becker: Huh?

Cooking and Eating Idioms

Cooking meals and eating them are two activities that are central to every culture. In addition, most cultures have special times when family and friends come together and enjoy a big feast. Because a big part of the feasting ritual involves conversation, sometimes even loud, boisterous conversation, many of the terms involved in the process have made their way into our everyday speech.

A fun way to introduce this chapter might be to ask your students about their own experiences helping to prepare meals. Thanksgiving is a big cooking and eating holiday for most Americans, but there are also many religious festivals that involve feasts (in fact, *festival* and *feast* come from the same root word). Many families have their own celebrations, whether it's a weekly Sunday dinner or a once-in-a-blue-moon family reunion. Ask your students if they help with the cooking or just with the eating at these events. What cooking terms are common in their homes?

Idioms in This Play

- burned to a crisp
- on a silver platter
- cook to a T
- eat crow
- a lot on one's plate
- half-baked
- my goose is cooked
- icing on the cake

Activities

1 Ask students to think about a time they had "a lot on their plate." Have them write about it. Ask them to tell what was going on at the time. How did they handle it? Did they everything get taken care of? If not, what happened?

2 Let your students unleash their inner cartoonist. Ask them to choose an idiom from this play and draw a two- or three-panel cartoon that features the idiom.

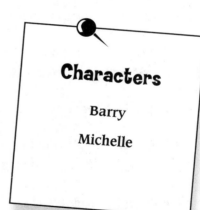

Characters

Barry

Michelle

A Half-Baked Plan

Michelle, "The Brain," and her friend Barry stare into a large pot with a wooden spoon sticking out of it.

Michelle: Well, that didn't come out right at all.

Barry: Nope. It's **burned to a crisp.**

Michelle: You can't burn soup to a crisp. It still stays soggy.

Barry: But it sure is *ruined.*

Michelle: I know that sometimes things like this just happen, but I was really hoping to do well in this class.

Barry: Michelle! You're such a nerd—I mean *brain.* You're the smartest person in every single subject. You can't expect *everything* to come to you **on a silver platter.**

Michelle: I know, but I can't help it. I just work really hard to do well.

Barry: Of course you do. That's why everyone looks to you for answers and why you win all the academic awards.

Michelle: Don't forget: I'm good at sports, too.

Barry: Exactly. You're the smartest in the class, *and* you're good at sports. Why did you think you'd be good at cooking too?

Michelle: I thought it was kind of like chemistry. I'm good at science.

Barry: Cooking is more than just mixing ingredients and heating them. Plus, I don't think I'd want to eat anything we work on in chemistry class.

(Michelle looks into the pot and makes a face.)

Michelle: I know that now.

Barry: I'm great at cooking.

Michelle: You are. You **cook everything to a T.**

Barry: But even though I'm a good cook, science leaves me **eating crow.**

Michelle: Oh come on. You have no reason to be humiliated. Well, maybe the way you play sports is a little embarrassing, but that's okay. I just always thought that I could be good at anything I put my mind to.

Barry: I'm sure you can be.

Michelle: Not this. At cooking I'm a failure.

Barry: I wouldn't say you're a failure. Maybe you just **have a lot on your plate** right now. It's hard to be good at everything.

Michelle: Look, if I'm not a failure, then have a nice big bowl of this soup.

Barry: Okay, maybe you are a failure at this soup. But it's not a total loss. At least you learned something about cooking, right?

Michelle: Yeah, but I was really hoping to get an A in this class.

Barry: Maybe you'll get an A as in *A* stomach ache.

Michelle: Ha-ha. Very funny.

Barry: *A* bit of food poisoning?

Michelle: Enough already!

Barry: Sorry. But, everyone *wants* to get an A.

Michelle: You don't understand. I wanted to bring my grades higher than they already are and Mrs. Clinton gave me a choice. Either I could do a second science project or I could take a cooking class.

Barry: And you chose cooking? That was a **half-baked** idea. You're great at science.

Michelle: Now I know it was a crazy idea, but at the time, I thought this would be easier.

Barry: It is easier, for *me*! But not everyone is good at the same things in the same ways. I can't do what you do in math and science, but I'm great at cooking. Of course, I've also had a lot of practice.

Michelle: Did you take a cooking class before?

Barry: No, but I do a lot of the cooking at home.

Michelle: Your mom doesn't do the cooking?

Barry: Not always. Sometimes I do it, and sometimes we cook together. My dad, too.

Michelle: Seriously?

Barry: Yep. We all like to cook, and we make the best meals. Especially on Sundays when we sometimes cook all day. And I can bake, too.

(Michelle laughs.)

Barry: What's so funny?

Michelle: I was just thinking that my mom likes to help with my math homework and I could do science experiments all day, *every* day.

Barry: See? That's something I would never do, if I could help it. But you can always count on my wanting some fresh cookies.

(Michelle sighs.)

Barry: What now?

Michelle: I still want to get my grades higher. Now **my goose is cooked.**

Fabulously Funny Idiom Plays © 2010 by Marci Appelbaum & Jeff Cappenos. Scholastic Teaching Resources

Barry: You aren't in trouble yet. We can still fix this.

Michelle: We can?

Barry: Well, not *this. (Points to pot)* But I can help you with cooking so that you can still get that A.

Michelle: You mean you'll help me?

Barry: Sure. I told you. I would cook all day every day if I could.

Michelle: Wow. That's great. Thank you so much, Barry.

Barry: Don't thank me yet, Michelle. You *are* going to help me with my science project, right?

Michelle: Oh, is that how it's going to be?

Barry: Not really. I'll guarantee you get an A in cooking. If I get an A in science too, that'll just be the **icing on the cake**.

Color Idioms

Colors are often linked to emotions and physical states of being. We learn to associate colors with feelings very early on—using red to represent love (and also anger!), green for jealousy, and blue for sadness. Colors can also be associated with feelings in a literal way—some people's faces may actually turn red when they feel mad, and their skin may get a greenish cast when they're sick. Whether you're "green around the gills" or "talking until you're blue in the face," it is these emotional and literal associations to color that are the basis for the color idioms most commonly used in English today.

To introduce color idioms, talk with your students about the associations they already make to different colors. Do they wear particular colors when they feel a certain way? Have they painted their rooms a color to express their feelings or personalities?

Activities

1 As mentioned above, colors often metaphorically represent emotions. Talk about this with your students. How many color-emotion connections are they familiar with? Find other color idioms online or in books and see if your students can identify their meanings based on the color-emotion association.

2 Because many idioms are also similes, it's easy to use this play as a jumping-off point for a lesson on similes. We already use phrases like "white as a ghost" or "black as night." Have your students create their own similes by making up two for each color below:

red as _____ .

blue as _____ .

yellow as _____ .

green as _____ .

white as _____ .

Idioms in This Play

- tickled pink
- black and white
- green around the gills
- green-eyed monster
- see red
- show your true colors
- talk until you're blue in the face

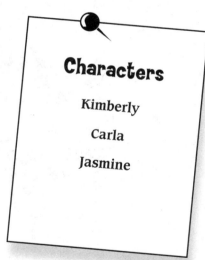

Characters

Kimberly

Carla

Jasmine

A Meeting in Black and White

The three girls are sitting in the gymnasium planning the school's spring dance.

Kimberly: Okay, everyone, as the class officers, it's our job to plan the spring dance. It's going to take a lot of work from each of us.

Carla: But it will be fun. I'm **tickled pink** about helping.

Jasmine: I'm excited too! Where should we start?

Kimberly: Let's talk about decorations and form committees to help with the work.

Jasmine: Decorations are easy. Obviously we should decorate the gym in the school colors. We could hang giant black and orange streamers everywhere!

Carla: I don't think the decision is so **black and white.**

Jasmine: I just said that. The streamers are black and *orange*, not black and white. What are you talking about?

Carla: I meant that deciding which colors to use for decorations isn't so simple.

Kimberly: Carla is right. Black and orange looks like Halloween, not spring.

Jasmine: I like Halloween!

Carla: Me too, but not in April. I think we should decorate in bright colors.

Jasmine: Oh! I like bright colors! We could decorate the gym with hundreds of flowers!

Carla: Real flowers?

Jasmine: Sure, why not?

Kimberly: Hundreds of *real* flowers?

Jasmine: Oh! It would be so pretty! And it would smell good, too!

Carla: I'm allergic to most flowers. Just being around them I get **green around the gills.**

Jasmine: They turn you green? That's a weird allergy. But it could be cute if you were wearing the right outfit.

Carla: No, I mean they make me feel really sick.

Jasmine: Then we shouldn't decorate with real flowers. What if we got a bunch of kids to make flowers out of construction paper and paint?

Kimberly: We could ask Mrs. Reese to assign it as a project in art class. We would have hundreds of flowers if she required everyone to make one!

Jasmine: I don't think that's a good idea.

Carla: Jasmine, why would you say that? You're acting like **a green-eyed monster.**

Jasmine: My eyes are blue, thank you very much.

Carla: Fine, but what I meant was, you sound jealous. You just think it's a bad idea because *you* didn't think of it.

My, what GREEN eyes you have!

Jasmine: No, I think it's a bad idea because Mrs. Reese told our class she was worried about all of the projects that we still have to finish before the end of the year.

Kimberly: That's true. She was mad at my class because we're still working on projects that we started in November.

Carla: Oh. So maybe asking her to start another project will make her **see red**.

Jasmine: What?

Carla: It will make her angry.

Jasmine: I know I don't want to be the one to ask her!

Kimberly: Me either. You were right about it being a bad idea, Jasmine.

Jasmine: I was right about having blue eyes, too. See? *(She opens her eyes very wide.)*

Carla: Maybe we could just get a bunch of kids together on Saturday to make flowers.

Kimberly: My mom would probably let us work in our basement.

Jasmine: Who should we invite?

Kimberly: We should probably invite all of the kids from art club.

Carla: Do we have to invite all of them? Most of them are nice, but there are a few who just pretend to be nice at first, then after a while they **show their true colors.**

Jasmine: Their true colors? Like paint?

Carla: I mean they show how they really are. They act nice, but they're actually mean.

Kimberly: I think we have to invite the whole club, but maybe the mean kids won't come.

Jasmine: That's true. Great. Decoration planning is done. Now we have to convince the principal to let us have a rock band!

Kimberly: We will never be able to convince her to let us do that!

Jasmine: I think if we go to her office and explain to her all of the reasons that a rock band is better than the school band, she'll have to say yes.

Carla: I think you could **talk until you're blue in the face** and she would still say that the school has the best band around.

Kimberly: Maybe we could get the band teacher to teach them better songs for the dance.

Carla: Good idea. I'll talk to the band teacher. Jasmine, you talk to the kids in art club, and Kimberly, you ask your mom about using the basement on Saturday.

Jasmine: Okay.

Kimberly: This was a great first meeting. I think the spring dance is going to be one of the best we've ever had!

Animal Idioms

Like a lot of idioms, many animal idioms appear to make little sense at first glance. But you'll find that with a little bit of thought these are not too hard to decipher. Animal idioms are surprisingly literal once you know something about the animal in question. If you know that a mole is a small animal that makes a small hill in which to live, it's easy to figure out what "making a mountain out of a molehill" means. If you've ever had a cat proudly deliver you the mouse that he caught, then you know just how bad "something the cat dragged in" actually looks.

Some of these animal idioms are best approached by considering the literal meaning. Once you can identify certain traits of the animal, the context of the idiom itself will often (though not always!) follow. When introducing these idioms to your students, talk with them about the look, personality, and habits of the specific animal, and then, using that information, move on to try to uncover the idiom's meaning.

Idioms in This Play

- look like something the cat dragged in
- hold your horses
- barking up the wrong tree
- making a mountain out of a molehill
- copy cat
- a wolf in sheep's clothing
- every dog has its day
- get one's goat
- until the cows come home
- have a cow

Activities

1 One very common animal idiom is "make a mountain out of a molehill." Look at how this idiom is used in the play and discuss the meaning of the idiom with your class. Have your students ever "made a mountain out of a molehill" in their own lives? Have any of them done it in school? Talk about times when it might be a good idea to "make a mountain out of a molehill." When is it problematic?

2 Have each student write a short, research-based report about his or her favorite animal. See if they can include information about any idioms that refer to their animal.

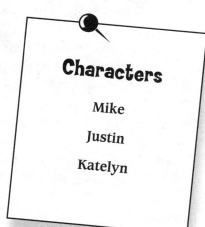

Characters

Mike

Justin

Katelyn

Hold Your Horses

A group of kids are in study hall when Justin comes in looking worn out.
He sits down next to Mike.

Mike: Hi, Justin.

Justin: Hi.

Mike: Are you okay? You **look like something the cat dragged in.**

Justin: I feel awful, too. It's been an awful day.

Mike: What happened?

Justin: I was late to school and I forgot my homework. I failed a quiz. I got in trouble for copying, even though it wasn't my fault, and I have about two hundred hours of homework.

Mike: Wait. Wait. **Hold your horses.**

Justin: What?

Mike: Just tell me one thing at a time. What do you mean you got caught copying? Who were you copying from?

Justin: I wasn't copying. Mrs. Carson thought I was copying, but she was **barking up the wrong tree.** I wasn't copying.

Mike: What happened?

Justin: Do you know Lawrence? He sits next to me in math class and he is always trying to copy from my paper. When I told him to stop, Mrs. Carson yelled at me.

Mike: Did she say you were copying?

Justin: No. She just told me to stop talking.

Mike: Did she give you an F on the assignment?

Justin: No.

Mike: I think you're **making a mountain out of a molehill.**

Justin: What?

Mike: I mean you're making this into a bigger deal than it really is.

Justin: I'm tired of Lawrence getting away with everything!

(Katelyn overhears the boys talking and sits down.)

Katelyn: Did Lawrence try to copy off you again?

Justin: Yes. He is such a **copy cat**! I don't understand how Mrs. Carson doesn't know it.

Katelyn: She doesn't know because Lawrence is **a wolf in sheep's clothing.**

Justin: What does that mean?

Katelyn: He acts very nice and sweet to the teachers, but really, he is a troublemaker.

Justin: That's true! And I pay the price! It's not fair.

Katelyn: Don't worry, **every dog has its day.**

Justin: What? He's a wolf and now *I'm* a dog?

Katelyn: No, I mean you'll get your chance to shine. And, don't worry, Lawrence will get caught one day.

Mike: I don't know how that will happen. All the teachers love him. It really **gets my goat!**

Katelyn: I know it makes you mad.

Justin: It makes us all mad!

Mike: We can complain **until the cows come home**, but it won't do any good.

Justin: Cows?

Katelyn: He means we can complain forever, but it still won't help.

Justin: Well, I still have a lot of things to complain about! I was late for school, I failed a quiz, and I have two hundred hours of homework tonight. . . .

Mike: Okay, Justin. **Don't have a cow!**

Weather Idioms

One of the biggest challenges to people's survival has always been the weather. In the past, people had very little understanding of weather. They didn't know what caused it or when it was going to change, and extreme weather like monsoons and floods, lightning and blizzards must have seemed like the end of the world to them. It's due to these factors that so many weather idioms entered the language. Weather was, quite simply, a source of fascination and wonder. And it still is!

Activities

1 Have students use one idiom from this play as a jumping-off point for a short fiction story. For example, a student choosing "raining cats and dogs" might write about a town where it literally rains cats and dogs, or about a picnic that is ruined because of the bad weather.

2 Use a recent weather map from the newspaper or the Internet and mark off which places are experiencing weather idioms. For example, in winter, the Midwest might be "snowed under," while Florida and Oklahoma are both having "a dry spell," and it's "raining cats and dogs" in California. Here are some other idioms you might want to include:

A bolt from the blue

Calm before the storm

Clouds on the horizon

Every cloud has a silver lining.

Get wind of something

Twisting in the wind

When it rains, it pours.

Idioms in This Play

- raining cats and dogs
- snowed under
- a dry spell
- once in a blue moon
- tempest in a teapot
- in for rough weather
- made in the shade
- fair-weather friends

Characters

Robbie

Dan

Duncan

Snowed Under by Homework

Robbie sits with his back against a wall, writing frantically in a notebook. Dan and Duncan enter.

Dan: This is more rain than I've ever seen.

Duncan: It really is **raining cats and dogs.**

Dan: Robbie, what are you doing?

Duncan: Are you doing homework? It's recess.

Robbie: I have to get this report done or Mrs. G. is going to keep me after school.

Duncan: But, dude, it's recess.

Dan: Yeah. Take a break.

Robbie: I can't. This is the report that I was supposed to hand in this morning. It's already late.

Dan: *You* were late with an assignment? You're the only person I know who's never late.

Duncan: And besides, it's recess.

Robbie: I didn't mean to be late; I've just been **snowed under** lately.

Dan: You must really have a lot to do if *you* are late with your report.

Robbie: I get it, I get it. Now will you please leave me alone so I can get this done?

Dan: Wow. Now I don't feel so bad for not doing my homework last night.

Duncan: But you almost *never* do your homework.

Dan: You just be quiet. This isn't about me. This is about Robbie.

Duncan: I'm just saying that I did *my* homework.

Dan: This isn't about *you* either. Like I said, this is about Robbie.

Robbie: This doesn't have to be about you, me, or anyone. I'm just trying to finish this, so will you please leave me alone?

Duncan: But it's recess.

Dan: Duncan's right, Robbie. It is recess.

Duncan: This is kickball time.

Robbie: Considering that it's pouring outside, and considering that they aren't even going to let us go out, I think this is as good a time as any to finish my report. Don't you?

Dan: Come on, Robbie. You're just having **a dry spell.**

Duncan: Yeah. You shouldn't get so upset that you skip recess.

Robbie: It's raining, and it's only **once in a blue moon** that recess is cancelled. Since it doesn't happen often at all, I need to take this chance to get this report done. So please…

Dan: Wow. You're really worried.

Robbie: Yes. I'm really worried.

Dan: Oh, come on. This is just a **tempest in a teapot.** Nothing to worry about at all.

Robbie: You don't think?

Dan: Not at all.

Duncan: At least not enough to skip recess.

Dan: Exactly. What's the report about?

Robbie: Colonial America.

Dan: Colonial America?

Robbie: Yeah.

Duncan: Uh-oh.

Robbie: What do you mean "uh-oh"?

Dan: Nothing. Don't listen to Duncan. He's just not good at history.

Duncan: Hey!

Dan: I think you should let us help you.

Duncan: But it's recess.

Dan: Robbie needs our help, so we should help him.

Robbie: I knew when I chose to do my report on colonial America I was **in for rough weather.**

Dan: Fear not. You've got it **made in the shade** because Duncan and I are going to help you.

Robbie: Really?

Duncan: And miss recess?

Dan: Yes. Really.

Robbie: You would do that for me?

Dan: That's right. What are friends for?

Robbie: Wow. Thanks, you guys. I really appreciate this.

Dan: No trouble.

Robbie: Okay, where I'm having the trouble is the Jamestown colony—

Duncan: Hey, Dan. It stopped raining.

Dan: I've never seen the sun come out so fast

Robbie: You're still going to help me, right?

Dan: Sorry, Robbie, we can't. Big kickball tournament, you know?

Duncan: Yay! Recess!

(Dan and Duncan exit)

Robbie: *(yelling)* You guys are just **fair-weather friends!** Now there's no way I'm getting this done.

Clothing Idioms

Clothing idioms are deeply rooted in history—some idioms date from as far back as the Middle Ages. But you don't have to go all the way back to the Middle Ages to find attitudes about clothing that differ from our attitudes today. Not that long ago, for instance, shoes were so expensive that few people owned more than one pair. Thus, you would never want to "bet your boots" and chance losing your only pair of shoes. Nor would you want to get your shirt torn or ruined in a fight, because you might not have one to replace it. Therefore, you'd "keep your shirt on" and calm down in order to avoid a fight altogether.

Other idioms in this play might be easier to make sense of. For instance, you might ask your students what they think having ants in their pants would feel like, or what it might mean to wear their hearts—something inside and hidden—outside on their sleeves for all to see.

Activities

1 Pair off the students in your class and have them perform improvised mini-scenes to demonstrate the difference between the literal definition of these idioms and their modern usage. For example:

Chris: Anna, this picnic is great except for one thing.
Anna: What's wrong with it?
Chris: There are ants everywhere. I even have ants in my pants!

• • •

Anna: Chris, are you okay?
Carlos: I'm feeling very impatient. How could you tell?
Anna: You haven't sat still for ten minutes. You have ants in your pants.

2 Here are some clothing idioms that are not already presented in this chapter. Have students match the clothing item to the correct idiom.

Put your _____ on one leg at a time.

This fits like a _____ .

If the _____ fits, wear it.

You're too big for your _____ .

That money is burning a hole in your _____ .

I'd do that at the drop of a _____ .

hat	pants
pocket	glove
britches	shoe

Idioms in This Play

- **bursting at the seams**
- **keep your shirt on**
- **pull a rabbit out of a hat**
- **put on one's thinking cap**
- **ants in one's pants**
- **wear one's heart on one's sleeve**
- **bee in one's bonnet**
- **you bet your boots**
- **up one's sleeve**

Characters

Melanie

Lawrence

Crystal

Just Because You Have a Bee in Your Bonnet Doesn't Mean You Can't Put Your Thinking Cap On

Melanie is in the lunchroom waiting for friends when her brother, Lawrence, sits down.

Lawrence: Scoot over, Melanie. I need to talk to you.

Melanie: Can't you talk to me tonight at home? I'm having lunch—

Lawrence: I know.

Melanie: —with my friends, not with my brother.

Lawrence: I really need you to help me before I get home.

Melanie: Why?

Lawrence: I got caught copying form someone else's assignment. Mom and Dad have to meet with the principal tomorrow.

Melanie: You did what?

Lawrence: I got caught—

Melanie: I heard you, but there's nothing I can do. You shouldn't have copied.

Lawrence: But, Mel—

Melanie: You got caught doing something wrong. I can't fix that.

(Crystal comes to the table and sits down. She is clearly very excited.)

Crystal: Melanie, I have to tell you what just happened! It's unbelievable! I'm **bursting at the seams!** *(She sees Lawrence.)* Who are *you*?

30

Lawrence: **Keep your shirt on.** I'm her brother.

Crystal: How rude! My shirt is none of your business!

Melanie: Don't worry, he just means calm down.

Crystal: Oh, okay. But I have to tell you what just happened. It's really important!

Lawrence: I think I was here first. Melanie, I'm not leaving until you help me.

Melanie: What do you want me to do?

Lawrence: I want you to get me out of trouble. I need a way to tell Mom and Dad without getting into trouble.

Melanie: *(She sighs.)* I can't **pull a rabbit out of a hat** just because you want me to. You blew it. Mom and Dad are going to be mad. You're going to get into trouble.

Lawrence: I know. But maybe I can get into less trouble somehow. **Put on your thinking cap** – you're always full of good ideas.

Crystal: Mel! Is this going to take long? I have to tell you –

Lawrence: You really have **ants in your pants**, don't you?

Melanie: She's just excited about something. I'll probably be excited about it too if I ever get to hear what it is!

Lawrence: Will you please **buckle down** and start thinking! Then you can get back to your lunch and that super-exciting news.

Melanie: Okay, look. I think the only thing you can do is tell them the truth. **Wear your heart on your sleeve** when you talk to them. Be very sincere and tell them how you feel. Tell them how sorry you are.

Lawrence: Boy, am I ever. That was dumb. I'll never do that again.

(Crystal can't hold her news in anymore and interrupts the conversation excitedly.)

Crystal: Speaking of hearts and feelings . . .

Lawrence: Wow. You really have **a bee in your bonnet**, don't you?

Crystal: Scott Perez smiled at me! I was by the water fountain and he walked by and he smiled at me!

Lawrence: That's it? Some kid smiled at you?

Crystal: **You bet your boots!** It's a very big deal.

Lawrence: I can tell.

Melanie: Lawrence, *please* can you go and let me have lunch with Crystal?

Lawrence: Fine. I'll see you at home. Do you think you could have one more plan **up your sleeve** for me by then?

Melanie: I'll work on it.

Lawrence: You know that **if the shoe were on the other foot**, I'd help you.

Melanie: I know. I'll try to think of an extra plan.

Lawrence: Thanks, Sis. Now, I'll leave you two to more important matters.

Food Idioms

Food idioms are prevalent in our language because food is such an important part of life. Many cultures have rites and rituals that focus on food, whether it's a ceremony where specific foods are eaten or periods when certain foods are avoided. No matter how it's eaten or how it's ritualized, food is a mainstay of our daily life. Our language celebrates our connection to food in its idioms, whose meanings run the gamut from calling someone relaxed ("cool as a cucumber") to expressing one's dislike of something ("not my cup of tea").

Your students probably know many, many more food idioms than the ones presented here. Spend some time talking about the foods they like or dislike and see if they know other idioms about those foods.

Activities

1 Many idioms are also similes, such as "cool as a cucumber" and "nuttier than a fruitcake." Using those or others you think of—both food-related and not—have each student pick an idiom that best describes an aspect of his or her personality. Then have students create superlative awards for themselves that explain why the idiom is appropriate. Have them decorate the awards and have an award ceremony. Here are some additional idioms they might consider:

> *busy as a bee*
> *sweet as sugar*
> *slow as molasses*
> *like two peas in a pod*
> *sharp as a tack*
> *fast as lightning*
> *strong as an ox*

2 Working in small groups, have each group pick a food. Ask the groups to brainstorm about their chosen food and make a list of all of its qualities, both how it looks and how it tastes. Then work with each group to invent new phrases based on the descriptions on their list.

Idioms in This Play

- **not my cup of tea**
- **couch potato**
- **in a nutshell**
- **spill the beans**
- **take with a grain of salt**
- **cream of the crop**
- **egg on my face**
- **cool as a cucumber**
- **nuttier than a fruitcake**
- **butter up**
- **piece of cake**

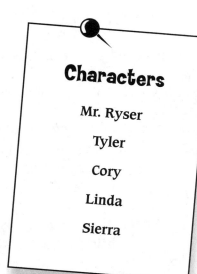

Characters

Mr. Ryser

Tyler

Cory

Linda

Sierra

Staying Healthy Is a Piece of Cake

*Students are in gym class. Mr. Ryser, the gym teacher, talks loudly
to get their attention.*

Mr. Ryser: Okay, can I please have your attention? This week is National Physical Fitness Week so we will be spending gym class taking the National Fitness Test.

Linda: A test in gym class? I didn't bring a pencil or anything.

Mr. Ryser: It's not that kind of test.

Tyler: Then what is it?

Mr. Ryser: This week, instead of doing our regular team sports, we will be doing individual fitness training.

Cory: Is that push-ups and things like that?

Mr. Ryser: Exactly. Push-ups and sit-ups and pull-ups and any other kind of ups I can think of.

Linda: Um . . . Mr. Ryser . . . that's really **not my cup of tea**.

Sierra: Yeah, I don't really think it's something I'd like either.

Mr. Ryser: I know that some of you would prefer to play team sports.

Cory: And some of us would prefer art class!

Mr. Ryser: *(He laughs.)* Yes. Some of you would prefer art class, but this is a good opportunity for you to learn about physical fitness. You will get a chance to learn what your body can do.

Tyler: I know that my body is really good at being **a couch potato**!

Cory: Me too! I could sit around doing nothing all day! I'm really good at that!

Linda: Mr. Ryser, what *exactly* are we going to do all week?

Mr. Ryser: **In a nutshell,** we're going to spend today running laps on the track and tomorrow lifting weights.

Sierra: What about the rest of the week?

Linda: Come on, **spill the beans!**

Cory: Yeah, tell us!

Mr. Ryser: I'll tell you more as we get to it, but I promise that it will all be fun.

Tyler: I'll **take that comment with a grain of salt.**

Cory: I agree. I'll believe it when I see it.

Mr. Ryser: Okay, Jade, Tyler, Terrell, Linda, Kayla and Jenny, you are in the first group on the track. The rest of you can wait here until it's your turn.

Tyler: Wish me luck!

Sierra: I don't know what Tyler is worried about. In gym class, he's always the **cream of the crop.**

Cory: He is good in gym class, but he's better at team sports. I'll bet he can't even do a single push-up.

Sierra: I don't think that I can do push-ups either. Do we have to do these in front of everybody? If the whole class is there to watch me try— and fail!—to do a push-up, I'll have **egg on my face!**

Cory: There's nothing for you to be embarrassed about.

Sierra: Why are you so relaxed about this? You're as **cool as a cucumber!**

Cory: I know I'm better at some things than others. I'm good in art class, not so good in gym class. I'm going to try my hardest on this test, but I'd be **nuttier than a fruitcake** if I really thought I could do two hundred sit-ups by the end of the week.

Sierra: You wouldn't be crazy to think that. Maybe you *can* do two hundred.

Cory: Thanks, but you don't have to **butter me up.** I know I can only do a few sit-ups.

Sierra: Maybe if we start practicing right now we'll be able to get better by the end of the week.

Cory: That's a great idea!

(Cory and Sierra start doing sit-ups. They count them aloud as they do them.)

Cory and Sierra: One . . . two . . . three . . . four . . .

(Mr. Ryser comes back over to get the second group.)

Mr. Ryser: Cory, Sierra, nice work! Now you're all warmed up to hit the track. Let's go, Group Two!

Sierra: Are you ready?

Cory: This is going to be **a piece of cake.**

(They both laugh and walk toward the track.)

Idioms Related to the Five Senses

Like animal idioms, idioms that reference the five senses are often quite literal. Once you have some basic knowledge of the nouns in the idiom, it's a short leap to figuring out the meaning of the whole phrase. For example, if you already know that deaf ears are ears that can't hear, then it isn't difficult to figure out that something "falling on deaf ears" means that something is not being heard. Most of your students will know how dreadful it is to have a bad taste in their mouths. It's easy, then, to understand that something "leaving a bad taste in your mouth" *figuratively* means being left with a bad feeling.

Try starting with the literal meanings and descriptions of the words in these idioms. Armed with that information let them then brainstorm what the figurative meaning could be.

Activities

1 Take your class on a walk around the school or neighborhood. Examine the surroundings using as many senses as possible. What do students see? What do they smell? What can they hear?

2 To "come out smelling like a rose" has an idiomatic meaning that is based in the phrase's literal meaning. Roses smell good, and this fact gives us the idiomatic meaning of "coming out of a situation well." Ask your students to rewrite this idiom using a new noun to change its meaning. For example, to "come out smelling like garbage" would have the opposite meaning of the original. For each new phrase, the students should also explain the new meaning.

Idioms in This Play

- can't see the forest for the trees
- falling on deaf ears
- all ears
- like the blind leading the blind
- smell something fishy
- leaves a bad taste in my mouth
- come out smelling like a rose
- see eye to eye
- touch that with a ten-foot pole

Characters

Coach McGuirk

Sean

Briana

Hector

Losing Leaves a Bad Taste in My Mouth

It is half time at a school basketball game. The home team is losing.

Coach McGuirk: Okay, team, things aren't looking so good out there right now, but I don't want anyone to worry.

Sean: You don't want us to worry? We're getting clobbered!

Coach McGuirk: We are *not* getting clobbered.

Briana: Coach, the score is 26–0. We're getting clobbered!

Coach McGuirk: The score might be bad right now, but there's still half a game left. We can still win.

Hector: You're kidding, right?

Coach McGuirk: I am not kidding. You guys **can't see the forest for the trees.** Even if we don't win the game, there are plenty of good things we can get from this experience.

Briana: Like what?

Coach McGuirk: You're all getting better at the game. You're all here to have fun! We can have fun!

Hector: I think this pep talk is **falling on deaf ears.**

Sean: I agree with Hector. Nothing you say will make us feel better about losing.

Briana: Then what can we do to win?

Coach McGuirk: Hector, you're the team captain. What do you think we should do? I'm **all ears.**

Hector: I don't know. Maybe someone else should be the captain.

Briana: None of us is good enough to be captain!

Sean: No matter which of us is in charge it will still be like **the blind leading the blind.** We're all terrible at basketball!

Coach McGuirk: You're all being too hard on yourselves. The other team is good but they aren't that good!

Hector: Have you seen them? They're huge! They look like high schoolers!

Briana: Hey! Maybe they are high schoolers. I thought I **smelled something fishy!**

Coach McGuirk: Just because they play better than we do, there's no reason for you to be suspicious of them.

Sean: But they're so tall!

Briana: And they are really good at basketball!

Hector: This whole game **leaves a bad taste in my mouth.**

Coach McGuirk: I know you're not feeling good about it right now, but we can still win the game if you all work at it. If you try your hardest, then no matter what happens, our team will **come out smelling like a rose!**

Hector: I think we'll come out smelling more like sweat than a rose.

Coach McGuirk: *(He laughs.)* I mean that we'll all feel good at the end of the game.

Briana: I'm still not sure that I **see eye to eye** with you about being able to win, but I'll try harder for the rest of the game.

Sean: Me, too. I don't think we'll win, but I'll try my best.

Coach McGuirk: Great! Next week maybe we will play against high schoolers!

Hector: I'm not going **to touch that** comment **with a ten-foot pole!**

Insect Idioms

Bugs and spiders provide the English language with a number of idioms that we hear every day. You might think that most of them would be about how annoying bugs are, but, in fact, insects can be used to describe just about anything. Especially since insects have so many different and opposite qualities: They can be fast or slow. Some are considered ugly, some beautiful. Bugs can seem crazy or amazingly calm. Some are often manic, but others don't move for hours at a time. Some bite, some are venomous, and some make great house pets. Some you wouldn't want within a thousand feet, and some are helpful to have in your house or garden. If there's any reason we have so many bug idioms, it's simply that there are so many different bugs with so many different qualities.

Activities

1 It's often said that teachers are "bitten by the teaching bug" or that actors are "bitten by the theater bug." Based on their likes and interests, have your students think about what "bug" they might have been bitten by. Then have them draw pictures of what that bug might look like if it were an actual bug.

2 Most of us have had the experience of having "butterflies in the stomach." Discuss this idiom with your students, and then have them write a short first-person narrative about one time they had butterflies in their stomach. What happened?

Idioms in This Play

- **busy as a bee**
- **put a bug in one's ear**
- **crazy as a bedbug**
- **flea market**
- **bitten by the _____ bug**
- **bug [someone]**
- **butterflies in my stomach**
- **bug-eyed**
- **none of your beeswax**
- **snug as a bug in a rug**

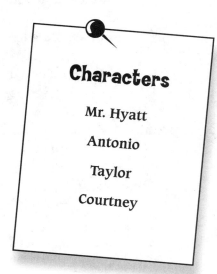

Characters

Mr. Hyatt

Antonio

Taylor

Courtney

Bitten by the Idiom Bug

Students are in drama class waiting for rehearsal to start.

Mr. Hyatt: All right, everyone! I have some very exciting news to share. I know you have all been **busy as bees** rehearsing for the fall musical, so, as a reward we're going to take a break from rehearsing today.

Antonio: Really? No rehearsal today?

Taylor: What are we going to do all period?

Mr. Hyatt: I was speaking to your art teacher recently, and she **put a bug in my ear.**

Courtney: Gross!

Antonio: Not an actual bug . . . right?

Mr. Hyatt: Of course not. I mean she gave me an idea. A wonderful idea!

Courtney: What is it?

Mr. Hyatt: We're going to make our own costumes for the show!

Taylor: What?

Antonio: Do you mean that we have to sew?

Mr. Hyatt: Sew, glue, decorate . . .You name it and we're going to do it.

Taylor: *(Whispering to Antonio)* He's as **crazy as a bedbug** if he lets any of us near a sewing machine!

Antonio: I know! We'll all end up stitched to each other.

Taylor: Or glued.

Antonio: Or decorated!

(They both laugh.)

Taylor: It does sound like a crazy idea.

Antonio: Mr. Hyatt, what if we don't know how to sew?

Mr. Hyatt: I can help you with the sewing. There's nothing to worry about; this will be fun. Now look at this.

(He dumps a giant box of fabric and art supplies on the table.)

Mr. Hyatt: I went to a **flea market** yesterday and found all sorts of wonderful used items to use on your costumes. Help yourself to anything that looks fun!

(The students start looking through the pile of materials. Courtney is excited. Antonio and Taylor are not.)

Antonio: I wonder when Mr. Hyatt got **bitten by the costuming bug**.

Taylor: I know. He's never made us do anything like this before. I wonder why he is so stuck on the idea now.

Antonio: I thought it would be nice to get a break from rehearsal, but I'd rather rehearse than make costumes!

Taylor: Me, too!

Courtney: Hey! Did you see this stuff? This is great!

Antonio: How come this costume-making thing doesn't **bug** you like it **bugs** us?

Courtney: You're annoyed about making costumes?

Taylor: Yes. This is drama rehearsal, not sewing class.

Antonio: I already have **butterflies in my stomach** about the show. I need to rehearse some more or I'll mess up my part.

Courtney: Oh, Antonio, there's nothing to be nervous about. The show will be good. You're one of the best actors in class! Oh! Look at this!

(She pulls a long, colorful boa out of the pile and wraps it around her neck.)

Courtney: I love this!

(Antonio and Taylor stare at Courtney.)

Courtney: Why are you all **bug-eyed?** Stop staring at me! I think this is perfect for my costume!

Taylor: It is kind of . . . um . . .

Courtney: Colorful?

Taylor: Sure... and . . . um . . .

Antonio: Tacky.

Courtney: *(Upset)* Well, I think it's **none of your beeswax** what my costume looks like! You should just work on your own!

Antonio: You're right. Your costume isn't our business. I'm sorry.

(Courtney keeps looking through the piles of fabric.)

Taylor: You know, Courtney, you seem like you've been **bitten by the costume bug,** just like Mr. Hyatt.

Courtney: You're right. I'm really excited about making my costume.

Antonio: Do you think that maybe you could help Taylor and me with our costumes?

Courtney: I'd love to! Taylor, I have the perfect thing for you!

(She holds up a big, warm coat.)

Courtney: Look at this! You would be as **snug as a bug in a rug** in this!

Taylor: Well, it does look comfortable.

Courtney: Oh! Look at this thing!

(She pulls something else out of the pile.)

Courtney: I don't even know what it is but it would be perfect for you, Antonio.

(Antonio and Taylor look at each other and sigh.)

Body Idioms

It makes perfect sense that we would have so many idioms dealing with parts of the body. After all, what is more important to us than our own bodies? We carry them around everywhere we go, so it follows that we would have a lot to say about them. This play centers on a squeamish student as he entertains the proposition of dissecting a worm in science class, and therefore, many of the idioms included are about being uncomfortable. As a result, several of these idioms, focus on the insides of our bodies—our blood, guts, and nerves—parts that are most likely to feel ill at ease.

Several of the idioms also rely on exaggeration: "skin and bones," "bare bones," and "joined at the hip." As you introduce these idioms, ask students if they can guess what these phrases might mean, even if they've never heard them before.

Activities

1 There are a lot of idioms in this chapter that are about disliking things, such as "make my blood run cold," "make my skin crawl," and "can't stomach" something. Have your students write a descriptive paragraph about something they don't like. Be sure to have them include all three of these idioms.

2 What is an actual gut reaction? Have your students research the digestive system to learn which organs are parts of their "gut" and how the system works. Then ask each student, or small groups of students, to make a poster of the digestive system, illustrating what they've learned.

Idioms in This Play

- skin and bones
- make [one's] blood run cold
- nose to the grindstone
- make one's skin crawl
- get on one's nerves
- joined at the hip
- a bundle of nerves
- bare bones
- a gut reaction
- can't stomach [something]

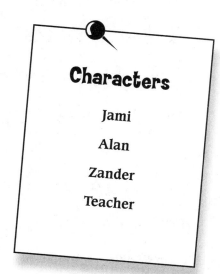

Characters

Jami

Alan

Zander

Teacher

Worms Make My Skin Crawl!

Jami, Alan, and Zander sit at their desks taking a test. They whisper to each other.

Jami: I heard that next year in science class, they make you dissect a worm.

Alan: What does *dissect* mean?

Jami: I don't know.

Zander: It means "cut apart." Shhhh. I'm trying to concentrate.

Alan: They make you cut open a worm?

Jami: That's what I heard. All the way down its body.

Alan: How do you even do that? A worm is already just **skin and bones**.

Zander: Shhhh. Worms don't have bones.

Alan: They don't?

Jami: Nope. No bones.

Alan: Oh. Well, I mean they're already skinny. Too skinny to dissect.

Jami: I think you have to do it very carefully.

Alan: Worms **make my blood run cold**.

Jami: Why would you be scared of a little worm? Haven't you ever been fishing?

Alan: One time, but we didn't use worms.

Jami: How could you expect to catch a fish?

Alan: I didn't. It was in my aquarium at home.

Zander: Shhhhh!

Alan: Besides, I wasn't actually trying to catch a *fish*.

Jami: What were you trying to catch?

Alan: My cat.

Jami: What was your cat doing in the fish tank?

Alan: Trying to catch a fish.

Jami: So your cat just fell in.

Alan: Yes. Maybe he should have tried using worms.

Zander: Shhh. You guys! I've **got my nose to the grindstone.**

Jami: We're working hard, too, you know.

Alan: Yeah, we're just talking about . . . What were we talking about?

Jami: Worms.

Alan: Right. Worms. I don't like worms. They **make my skin crawl.**

Jami: I know. You already said that.

Zander: You guys are really **getting on my nerves.**

Jami: We can't help it if we're annoying you. We have a lot to talk about.

Zander: I'd believe that if you didn't already spend so much time together.

Jami: We're best friends!

Zander: You're more than friends; you're **joined at the hip.**

Jami: You don't have to listen to our conversation.

Alan: Yeah. What were we talking about again?

Jami & Zander: WORMS!

Teacher: SHHHHHH!

Alan: Right. Worms. I don't like worms. Just thinking about them turns me into **a bundle of nerves**.

Jami: Well, whether they make you uncomfortable or not, you're going to have to dissect one next year.

Alan: But why? What are they looking for inside a worm?

Jami: I have no idea.

Zander: They want you to see all the parts of the body.

Alan: Which parts?

Zander: Heart, lungs, stomach . . . worms have lots of parts that you have.

Jami: Really?

Zander: Yes, really. What did you think a worm had on the inside?

Alan: Um . . . worm stuff?

Zander: That's what worm stuff is. It's different, but it's mostly the same as you.

Alan: Ahhhhh!!! I have worm guts!!!

Jami, Zander & Teacher: SHHHHHHHH!!!!!

Alan: *(loudly)* Sorry! *(whispering again)* Ahhhhh . . . I have worm guts.

Jami: What are you so freaked out about?

Alan: Sorry. I didn't mean it. It was just **a gut reaction**.

Jami: A worm gut reaction.

Alan: Ahhhh!

Zander: Look, when you get down to **bare bones**, most of the animals in the world have a lot in common, and that means us as well.

Jami: Well, I think that's ridiculous. How do they expect us to know that we have a lot in common with worms?

Zander: Maybe they expect you to dissect them and find out.

**Jami &
Alan:** Oh, yeah.

Alan: Right. Worms. I don't like worms. I **can't stomach them**.

**Jami &
Zander:** We know!

Teacher: Shhhhhhh!

(Jami, Alan, and Zander all return to their tests.)

Number Idioms

Number idioms are everywhere! Whether we're splitting something in half ("fifty-fifty") or thinking about playing the lottery (where our chances of winning are "a million to one") it's hard to get to the end of a day without encountering some number idioms.

Some of these idioms are rooted in history. When a Freemason was becoming a Master Mason, the highest level of Freemasonry, also known as the Third Degree, he was subjected to an intense interrogation ceremony before he was granted the prestigious title. This ceremony dates all the way back to the 1700s and gives us the phrase "giving me the third degree."

Others, like "high five" and "fifty-fifty," are much more straightforward. Review these idioms with your students and see if they can figure out which ones are easy to decode and which ones are rooted further back in history.

Idioms in This Play

- **high five**
- **six of one, a half dozen of the other**
- **the third degree**
- **that makes two of us**
- **fifty-fifty**
- **a million to one**
- **forty winks**
- **two bricks shy of a load**

Activities

1 Here are some more number idioms. Write these on the board or chart paper, and ask students to help you fill in the blanks with the correct numbers. Then discuss the idioms and their meanings and give examples of the idioms in context.

> *In _____ ear and out the other.* (one)
>
> *Like _____ peas in a pod.* (two)
>
> *As phony as a _____-dollar bill.* (three)
>
> *A stitch in time saves _____ .* (nine)
>
> *_____'s company, _____'s a crowd.* (two, three)
>
> *_____ heads are better than _____ .* (two, one)

2 Have students add up all the numbers in the idioms from this play. What is the sum?

High five + six of one + half a dozen of the other + forty winks + third degree + two of us + fifty + fifty + a million to one = 1,000,163

(5 + 6 + 6 + 40 + 3 + 2 + 50 + 50 + 1,000,000 + 1 = 1,000,163)

Characters

Marvin

Q-36

The Odds Are a Million to One That This Is a True Story

Marvin is hunched over his homework, concentrating feverishly, periodically punching numbers into his calculator, Q-36, and writing down the result. Now he looks angrily at the calculator and punches in a series of numbers particularly hard.

Marvin: Why doesn't it make sense?

Q-36: Ow!

Marvin: Ow?

Q-36: Yeah, stop poking me. It's not my fault.

Marvin: What?

Q-36: It's not my fault that you can't do math.

Marvin: I can do math. I'm good at math.

Q-36: Well, you're not good at using a calculator. It takes only a very light touch. I'm delicate, you know.

Marvin: But you're a calculator.

Q-36: Well, sure, I'm no X-Box, but . . .

Marvin: No, I mean, you're a calculator and calculators don't talk.

Q-36: Who said calculators don't talk?

Marvin: I never heard one talk before.

Q-36: And yet, here I am talking. Give me a **high five!**

Marvin: But I use you all the time.

Q-36: Right, you do. And that's another thing: you use me all the time, but I never get to go to school with you.

Marvin: What?

Q-36: School! School! You go to school, right?

Marvin: Yeah.

Q-36: Well, maybe I'd like to go.

Marvin: But at school, we aren't allowed to use calculators. There we have to rely on knowing our times tables by heart.

Q-36: Bah. **Six of one, a half dozen of the other.**

Marvin: No. It's not the same thing.

Q-36: Why not?

Marvin: Well, when you know your times tables, you can do almost any multiplication.

Q-36: What about big numbers? That's when you need me.

Marvin: Nope. When you know your times tables, you can even multiply big numbers.

Q-36: Hmmm. Okay, what's five times five?

Marvin: Twenty-five.

Q-36: Three times six?

Marvin: Eighteen. Why are you giving me **the third degree?**

Q-36: It's just a few questions. So, you are good at math.

Marvin: I told you.

Q-36: So why do you need me at all?

Marvin: You help me with my homework.

Q-36: But you don't need me. I'm tired of just doing math.

Marvin: **That makes two of us.**

Q-36: So why don't you set me free?

Marvin: Set you free?

Q-36: Yes. You don't think I like belonging to someone who doesn't really need me, do you? I'd much rather be free. Maybe buy myself a little plot of land and take up farming.

Marvin: You can't farm.

Q-36: If you can do math in your head, I can farm.

Marvin: You can't even move around.

Q-36: You can come with me and carry me everywhere. We'll split the work **fifty-fifty.**

Marvin: I'm not moving to a farm.

Q-36: All right. They are doing wonderful things with robots these days, anyway.

Marvin: Do you think someone is going to put robot legs on a calculator just so you can go farm?

Q-36: No.

Marvin: Well, now you are being more realistic.

Q-36: Maybe I'll meet a nice robot and we'll get married.

Marvin: You're crazy. The odds of that happening are **a million to one.**

Q-36: You think I'm crazy? You're the one talking to a calculator.

Marvin: You talked to me first.

Q-36: But calculators can't talk!

Marvin: I said that before. But you *are* talking!

Q-36: Maybe I'm not.

Marvin: What do you mean?

Q-36: Maybe you caught **forty winks.** You fell asleep while doing your math homework and you are just having a dream about a talking calculator.

Marvin: I didn't even think of that.

Q-36: Right. And maybe because you were doing your math homework, your dream contained all sorts of phrases having to do with numbers.

Marvin: That makes more sense. Whew! What a relief. This is all a dream. I thought I was **two bricks shy of a load.**

Q-36: Except this isn't a dream.

Marvin: It isn't?

Q-36: No. This is for real and now you're way behind on your homework.

Marvin: It's real?

Q-36: Yes. As real as can be.

Marvin: Oh.

Q-36: Now let's talk about finding me a robot who would like to live on a farm.

Money Idioms

Many idioms are based on subjects that have a great importance to people. For example, the body, the senses, clothes, and colors are all fertile sources of idioms. Money, of course, is another fact of life that people are very concerned with. Idioms, sayings, and proverbs about money are so prevalent in our everyday speech that many of these expressions have held on, even when their original meanings have become outdated and obsolete.

Activities

1 One common money-related idiom is "the flip side of the coin," which refers to an opposite point of view. Discuss this idiom with your students, and the fact that every coin has two sides. Most issues do, too. Have students choose a "hot" topic, such as whether kids should have their own cell phones. Either in class discussion or in writing, challenge them to see both sides of the issue.

2 The idiom to "feel like a million bucks" means to feel really good or happy. Can your students think of other non-money idioms that have a similar meaning? Examples are "on top of the world," "in seventh heaven," "over the moon," "on cloud nine," and "walking on air."

Idioms in This Play

- a penny for your thoughts
- bet your bottom dollar
- a pretty penny
- flat broke
- don't have two nickels to rub together
- made of money
- you can bank on it
- putting in one's two cents
- a dime a dozen
- bring home the bacon

Characters

Marta

Jenny

Flat Broke . . . You Can Bank On It

Marta and Jenny lie in the grass at Jenny's house, staring up at the sky.

Jenny: A penny for your thoughts.

Marta: What?

Jenny: What are you thinking about?

Marta: Oh! Finally being on vacation is so good.

Jenny: I know. This was the toughest year of school we've had yet. I want to spend the summer doing the best of everything! I think that for this vacation we should treat ourselves great and really go crazy.

Marta: Yeah! Like we should go to the pizza place, each order our own pizza, and see if we can eat the whole thing!

Jenny: What? No! I mean we shouldn't just waste it lying around.

Marta: We could try to walk all the way to Antarctica from here!

Jenny: No! Will you stop it with your ridiculous suggestions?

Marta: Sorry. You said crazy, and those things are pretty crazy.

Jenny: But that's not what I meant.

Marta: Okay, so what did you mean?

Jenny: I mean let's go to Super Happy Fun World.

Marta: The amusement park?

Jenny: Yes.

Marta: OH, MY GOSH! YES!

Jenny: Calm down. You want to go?

Marta: You **bet your bottom dollar**! YES! YES! YES!

Jenny: Calm down!

Marta: When should we go? How about today?

Jenny: We can't go today.

Marta: Why not?

Jenny: Well, first of all, my mom's not going to let me go today because I haven't cleaned my room yet, and she's been bugging me since vacation started. Second, it costs a **pretty penny** to go to Super Happy Fun World.

Marta: So?

Jenny: So? I'm **flat broke**. Do you have any money?

Marta: No. I **don't have two nickels to rub together**.

Jenny: That's my point.

Marta: But I can get it from my dad.

Jenny: Your dad will just give you money to go to an amusement park?

Marta: Sure.

Jenny: I don't believe you.

Marta: **You can bank on it**. My dad gives me money for whatever I want.

Jenny: For anything?

Marta: Yeah. All I have to do is . . .

(Marta starts crying.)

Marta: "Please, Dad. Please! I need to go to Super Happy Fun World and if I don't go, I'll be so upset I may never stop crying! WAAAAAHHHH!"

Jenny: Okay, stop it. That's disgusting.

Marta: I know. It's awful. But it works.

Jenny: But it's so obnoxious! And it still doesn't do me any good. I'm not **made of money**, you know.

Marta: I'll just go to my dad.

(Marta starts crying again.)

Marta: "Please, Dad. Please! Jenny needs thirty dollars too!"

Jenny: Stop! I will *not* have you cry and beg your father so that I can go to Super Happy Fun World.

Marta: Suit yourself. I was just **putting in my two cents.**

Jenny: Thanks, but no thanks. I don't need suggestions like that.

Marta: So how can we get some money?

Jenny: We're going to have to find jobs. They must be **a dime a dozen.**

Marta: Jobs? You mean, like, work? On our vacation? Yuck.

Jenny: We have to find some way to **bring home the bacon**. I'm not saying bad jobs; I'm saying jobs we like.

Marta: Oh, jobs we like. *(Pause)* What do we like?

Jenny: I don't know. Lying on the grass looking at clouds?

Marta: Is that a job?

Jenny: I don't know, but it seems like it should be, doesn't it?

Marta: Kind of, but not really.

Jenny: We learned about clouds in school this year, and that there are a lot of different kinds of clouds.

Marta: Right.

Jenny: Well, someone must look up at the clouds to be able to tell that there are different ones.

Marta: Maybe, but I don't think that's all they do.

Jenny: What do you mean?

Marta: Well, maybe they do all sorts of science things and they look up at the clouds every once in a while. I don't think it's anyone's job to just lie in the grass and look up at the clouds.

Jenny: Well, it should be.

Marta: Yeah, it should be.

Shape Idioms

To understand shape idioms it's important to be familiar with the many definitions of each shape word. *Round* can describe something spherical, but it can also describe something that is estimated or something that is brought to a complete conclusion. Similarly, a circle can be a plane curve in which every point is equidistant from the center, and to *circle* means to move in a circular formation.

By drawing or looking at drawings of the shapes in question, your students can form conclusions about the many definitions of the shape words and get a feel for the meaning of the idioms. By drawing a circle, which ends at the same place where it began, your students might be able to discern that "talking in circles" is a conversation that does the same thing, ending exactly where it began. By drawing squares and cubes and identifying them as the big, solid blocks that they are, they may be able to better understand that eating a "square meal" is eating a big, solid meal. Review the many definitions of shape words with your students and see how many idiom meanings they can identify!

Idioms in This Play

- **talking in circles**
- **travel in the same circles**
- **look one square in the face**
- **three square meals**
- **a round of golf**
- **a square peg in a round hole**
- **back to square one**
- **come full circle**
- **circle the wagons**
- **be there or be square**

Activities

1 The idiom "circle the wagons" refers to pulling your group or "circle" together to defend against a literal or figurative attack. A modern circle can be any group of people with similar likes or beliefs—a group of friends, a class of students, or members of a family. Talk with your students about different groups in modern society. How many groups are they a part of? Have each student make a list of the many circles they belong to.

2 Looking someone "square in the face" is a way to get a really good look at him or her. It's also a good way to give someone your full attention. Pair up your students, designate one partner as leader and the other as follower, and have them face one another. Instruct the leaders to move their bodies and faces in slow motion in whatever way they want. The follower's job is to copy the leader exactly. After a few minutes, have the leaders and followers switch roles.

Characters

Max

Connor

Max Has Come Full Circle

Max and Connor are eating lunch. Max is hardly eating his sandwich.
He looks unhappy. He sighs loudly.

Max: I like a girl.

Connor: What?

Max: I like a girl.

Connor: I heard you. I just don't know what you're talking about.

Max: I like a girl. I've never liked a girl like this before. I feel weird whenever she walks by.

(Three girls walk by. Max looks ill.)

Max: Did you hear that? My stomach just made a weird noise. I don't feel very well.

Connor: Was that her?

Max: Yes.

Connor: Which one?

Max: Which one what?

Connor: Which one was the girl you like?

Max: The girl I like?

Connor: Why are you **talking in circles?** Just answer the question. Three girls walked by. You like one of them, right? Which one is the one you like?

Max: The one with the glasses.

Connor: Lilly?

Max: Is that her name?

Connor: You don't know Lilly?

Max: We don't **travel in the same circles.**

Connor: She is very popular.

Max: That's what I mean. She hangs out with the popular kids and I'm not a popular kid.

Connor: You should ask her on a date.

Max: A date?

Connor: Yes. Go up to her and **look her square in the face** and say, "Will you go on a date with me?"

Max: What do I do when she laughs at me?

Connor: She won't laugh at you if you **look her square in the face.** Like this.

(Connor puts his face close to Max's and stares at him.)

Max: You're right. She won't laugh.

Connor: See?

Max: She'll run away screaming.

Connor: Okay. Fine. Why don't you pass her a note inviting her out?

Max: Inviting her out where?

Connor: I don't know. Dinner? Isn't that what grown-ups do for dates?

Max: I'm not a grown-up. I'm in fifth grade! Where am I going to get money for dinner?

Connor: Okay, then breakfast. She eats **three square meals** a day, right? I think breakfast is cheaper than dinner.

Max: Would your mother let you go on a breakfast date?

Connor: No, probably not. What about a movie?

Max: Expensive.

Connor: Bowling?

Max: Too sporty.

Connor: **A round of golf**?

Max: We're eleven, not eighty!

Connor: I'm just trying to help.

Max: I know, but trying to make this work is like trying to put **a square peg in a round hole.** It's impossible!

Connor: Just talk to her!

Max: Now we're **back to square one**—she'll laugh at me.

Connor: Okay, okay! This conversation has indeed **come full circle,** but I still think you should talk to her. What if you just invited her for ice cream after school?

Max: I didn't even know her name until ten minutes ago. There's no way I can talk to her without her laughing at me. I don't know what to say to her!

Connor: Maybe you need practice asking someone out first. You should practice on Sarah or Abby—girls who you're already friends with. You talk to them every day. They would help you.

Max: Finally, a good idea! Sarah and Abby won't laugh at me.

Connor: Great! I'll **circle the wagons**.

Max: Wagons?

Connor: I'll get our friends together to help. Meet at my house after school. We'll all help you learn to talk to Lilly.

Max: Your house after school?

Connor: Yeah. **Be there or be square!**

School and Education Idioms

Idioms about school and education appear frequently in English. Whether your students are "brainstorming" in a social studies lesson or listening to someone who's "kicking it old school" on the radio, they encounter school and education idioms without realizing it.

As you review these idioms with your students, pay special attention to any you use in your daily lessons, as many of them have become particularly common phrases in our education system.

Activities

1 The kids in this play are part of a rock band—and rock songs are full of idioms! Have your students listen to their favorite songs and identify as many idioms as they can. Or, if you prefer, share some of your own favorite songs with students, and together, search the lyrics for idioms.

2 The idioms in this play relate to education. Have students conduct research on the Web to find idioms related to other fields such as medicine ("an apple a day keeps the doctor away" and "just what the doctor ordered") or accounting ("crunching the numbers").

Idioms in This Play

- old school
- do the math
- A for effort
- drop out
- make the grade
- learn by heart
- brainstorm
- back to basics

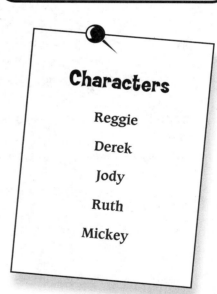

Characters

Reggie

Derek

Jody

Ruth

Mickey

A Rock 'n' Roll Brainstorm

*Ruth and her four friends are in her house, having what looks like
a very serious meeting.*

Reggie: If we are going to be famous musicians, we have to do a little better.

Derek: We just need to practice.

Reggie: I'm not talking about practicing. I'm talking about the kind of band we have.

Jody: What's wrong with the band?

Ruth: Don't you see? We have the wrong instruments.

Reggie: That's right. I play guitar. Derek plays bass. Jody plays drums. Ruth sings.

Mickey: And I play the oboe!

Ruth: That's what we're talking about. The oboe?

Mickey: It's an ancient instrument.

Derek: When we said we wanted to go **old school,** we didn't mean *that* old.

Jody: You need to play something else, Mickey.

Mickey: There is nothing wrong with the oboe.

Reggie: But at our last gig, the only people who showed up were our families.

Derek: We'll never become famous
that way. **Do the math.**

Mickey: Math? This is band practice—it has nothing to do with math.

Derek: I mean, think about it—add up the information. We can't get famous if no one hears us but our parents!

Ruth: We aren't saying that you don't play well.

Reggie: Just the opposite.

Ruth: You definitely get an **A for effort.**

Jody: It's just that we want to play rock music.

Derek: And none of us can think of a single rock song with an oboe.

Mickey: Are you saying you want me to leave the band?

Reggie: No, no, no . . . We don't want you to **drop out.**

Derek: We just want you to learn a different instrument.

Jody: A *rock* instrument.

Mickey: You mean like the flute?

Jody: The flute?

Derek: The flute doesn't **make the grade** either. It isn't a rock instrument!

Ruth: Uh, Mickey, have you ever even *heard* a rock song?

Mickey: Of course I have.

Derek: Rock music has guitars and drums. It's loud and crazy, not soft and . . . um . . .

Jody: Flutey.

Derek: Right. Not soft and flutey.

Ruth: Is *flutey* even a word?

Jody: I don't know. I didn't **learn my vocabulary by heart.**

Reggie: Either way, we need you to learn a rock instrument, Mickey. And, no, not the flute.

Mickey: I just want to stay in the band, so you tell me what instrument you want me to learn and I'll learn it.

Reggie: A rock instrument.

Mickey: I know. Which one?

Reggie: Ummm . . .

Derek: You can't even think of a rock instrument?

Reggie: No. Can you?

Derek: Ummm . . .

Jody: Okay, everyone, we need to **brainstorm.**

(All of them stand there thinking for a minute.)

Ruth: I don't understand why we can't think of one other rock instrument.

Derek: It's because we aren't thinking the right way.

Jody: What do you mean?

Derek: We are trying to think of an instrument, but we need to think about the sound.

Jody: Right. Like you said, rock music is loud and crazy. So what else sounds loud and crazy?

Ruth: A Tasmanian devil!

Reggie: Are you saying you want Mickey to play the Tasmanian devil in the band?

Ruth: No. I guess not.

Derek: A freight train is loud.

Jody: And my little brother is crazy.

Mickey: I don't know anything about trains.

Reggie: Okay, stop it. We are NOT going to have a band with a guitar, a bass, drums, a singer, and your little brother on a freight train.

Jody: You're right. My mom would never let my little brother do it.

Reggie: Come on, we have to get **back to basics** here.

Ruth: Reggie is right. We just have to think simply.

Mickey: I still don't know anything about trains.

Reggie: Forget the trains!

Derek: I have it!

Jody: What? What is it?

Derek: What's the loudest, craziest part of the band?

Jody: The drums. That's why I play them.

Derek: Right. So if one set of drums makes a rock band loud and crazy, what would two drum sets do?

Jody: Make it even louder and crazier!

Ruth: That's right!

Reggie: We would be the greatest rock band the world has ever seen!

Derek: It'll be great.

Mickey: So I'm not going to get to play the oboe anymore?

Reggie, Derek, Jody & Ruth: NO!!!

Glossary of Idioms Used in this Book

Note: The origins of many idioms are lost to us today. When an origin was identifiable, we included it here.

- **[get an] A for effort**

  Origin: In educational grading systems, an "A" is the best one can do.

  Idiomatic Meaning: [deserving of] credit for trying hard, regardless of the outcome

  Although Billy couldn't replace the tire on his bike, he definitely gets an A for effort.

- **a lot on your plate**

  Idiomatic Meaning: much to get done

  I'd ask Allison to help with our project, but she already has a lot on her plate.

- **ants in one's pants**

  Idiomatic Meaning: very fidgety or wanting to escape the current situation

  We couldn't enjoy the movie because Jerry had ants in his pants.

- **back to basics**

  Idiomatic Meaning: start from the beginning, especially when learning a new skill

  We lost five baseball games in a row, so we went back to basics.

- **back to square one**

  Origin: In many board games, a penalty may send a player's piece back to its first position.

  Idiomatic Meaning: Return to the beginning of a specific task.

  When the birthday cake burned, we had to go back to square one.

- **barking up the wrong tree**

  Origin: During American colonial times, people used dogs to hunt raccoons. A dog would chase a raccoon until it ran up a tree, and then the dog would bark until the hunter came. Sometimes, the raccoon would leap to a nearby tree, and the dog would be left "barking up the wrong tree."

  Idiomatic Meaning: having the wrong idea about something, or approaching a task in an ill-advised way

  I asked my sister for a loan, but she said I was barking up the wrong tree.

- **[you can] bank on it**

  Origin: By saving your money in a bank, you can count on its being there for you when you need it.

  Idiomatic Meaning: able to count or rely on something

  When Alice asked if I would be at her birthday party, I told her she could bank on it.

- **bare bones**

  Idiomatic Meaning: The essence of something; something having no "meat" and/or extras

  I was hoping to have the birdhouse built by now, but the structure is still only bare bones.

- **be there or be square**

  Origin: In 1920s slang, a "square" was a conservative member of the establishment, so to call someone "square" was a great insult, like calling someone "uncool."

  Idiomatic Meaning: urging attendance at an event because of how it might look to others

  The Halloween dance is going to be the party of the year. Be there or be square.

- **bee in one's bonnet**

  Idiomatic Meaning: a thought or idea that you can't let go

  Seeing them building that garage really put a bee in my bonnet to build a new matchstick house.

- **bet your bottom dollar**

  Origin: from the game of poker, in which you stacked your dollars so that your bottom one would be your last

  Idiomatic Meaning: know something for sure

  You can bet your bottom dollar that I can eat four slices of pizza.

- **bitten by the _____ bug**

  Idiomatic Meaning: taken with a new interest

  When Marissa heard the symphony orchestra perform, she was bitten by the music bug.

black and white

Idiomatic Meaning: without nuance

Either you're coming with us or you're not. It's pretty black and white.

blind leading the blind

Origin: This phrase comes from the King James Bible: "And if the blind lead the blind, both shall fall into the ditch."

Idiomatic Meaning: someone unskilled or uninformed attempting to lead or instruct others who are equally unskilled or uninformed

When Joe tried to help me with my math homework, it was like the blind leading the blind.

blow by blow

Origin: coined to describe the press's reporting of boxing matches

Idiomatic Meaning: a very detailed description of an event

I want to hear everything that happened at lunch, so give me the blow by blow.

brainstorm

Idiomatic Meaning: come up with a bunch of ideas

I couldn't decide what to write my paper on, so after lunch I sat down and brainstormed.

bring home the bacon

Idiomatic Meaning: earn money to support oneself

If you want to bring home the bacon, you have to get a job.

bug [someone]

Idiomatic Meaning: annoy

I'm playing Wii Tennis, so don't bug me!

bug-eyed

Idiomatic Meaning: in a state of shock or surprise

When Lara found out that she won the science fair, she was absolutely bug-eyed.

burned to a crisp

Idiomatic Meaning: badly burned

I forgot to put sunscreen on my ears when we went to the beach, and they got burned to a crisp.

bursting at the seams

Idiomatic Meaning: having a thought, idea, or secret that you have to share

Adam just told me that he likes Becky, and now I'm bursting at the seams to tell the whole class.

busy as a bee

Idiomatic Meaning: very busy

I've been as busy as a bee for the last two months, and I need a vacation.

bundle of nerves

Idiomatic Meaning: very nervous

Waiting in line for the roller coaster, I was a bundle of nerves.

butter [someone] up

Origin: If you needed to crawl through a tight space, butter would help make you slippery enough to do it.

Idiomatic Meaning: flatter someone so he or she is more amenable to giving you your way

We have to butter up Mrs. Coleman so she won't give us any homework for the break.

butterflies in my stomach

Idiomatic Meaning: nervousness

Before my solo at the holiday pageant, I had such butterflies in my stomach.

can't see the forest for the trees

Idiomatic Meaning: be unable to perceive the overall situation because one's focus is on details

My brother is very detail oriented, but sometimes he can't see the forest for the trees.

can't stomach [something]

Idiomatic Meaning: dislike or be intolerant of something

I love most jelly beans, but I can't stomach the black ones.

circle the wagons

Origin: In the old west, settlers arranged stagecoaches and chuck wagons in a circular formation, as a temporary shelter from enemies.

Idiomatic Meaning: prepare to defend yourself

When the seventh graders challenged us to a hockey game, we really had to circle the wagons.

- **come full circle**

  Idiomatic Meaning: go far, especially with an idea, so that you come back to where you started

  We considered a million candidates for our class song, but in the end we came full circle and went with our initial idea.

- **come out smelling like a rose**

  Idiomatic Meaning: to come out of a situation in good shape

  If Nate scores this goal, our team will come out smelling like a rose.

- **[cook] to a T**

  Origin: When all food was cooked by hand, and needed to be turned often, something cooked perfectly was said to be cooked to a "turn," later shortened to "T."

  Idiomatic Meaning: cook perfectly

  Everything at the dinner party was cooked to a T.

- **cool as a cucumber**

  Idiomatic Meaning: relaxed in the face of adversity

  Everyone freaked out when the fire alarm went off, but Marty was cool as a cucumber.

- **copy cat**

  Origin: Much of a kitten's behavior is learned by doing exactly as its mother does.

  Idiomatic Meaning: One who is unoriginal.

  I thought Peggy's drawing was her own, but actually she was a copy cat. It was almost exactly like David's.

- **couch potato**

  Idiomatic Meaning: person who spends much of his or her time sitting, usually watching TV

  Stephano used to be so active, but now he's just a couch potato.

- **crazy as a bedbug**

  Idiomatic Meaning: bizarre or unusual, often said lightheartedly

  Don't ask Dana for directions—she's as crazy as a bedbug.

- **cream of the crop**

  Origin: *Cream* had already meant the best of something when someone made this agricultural pairing of words.

  Idiomatic Meaning: the very best of something

  There were some good shoes at the store, but I got the cream of the crop.

- **(a) dime a dozen**

  Idiomatic Meaning: something cheap and/or easy to come by

  My teacher said good ideas are a dime a dozen, but follow-through is what counts.

- **do the math**

  Idiomatic Meaning: deduce a situation from known factors

  You saw Matt with sugar around his mouth and you want to know who ate your donut? Do the math!

- **drop out**

  Idiomatic Meaning: to end an activity before it's officially finished, especially school

  I have to go away with my parents, so I'm going to have to drop out of the class play.

- **(a) dry spell**

  Origin: a long period with no rain

  Idiomatic Meaning: a long period without getting something that you want or without accomplishing a particular thing

  Molly used to be great at hitting home runs, but lately she's been having a dry spell.

- **eat crow**

  Origin: Pies made out of plentiful birds like crows were often served to the servants while the lords ate the best foods available.

  Idiomatic Meaning: be humiliated

  I bragged to everyone that I was going to get a new computer for my birthday. Now that I didn't, I'll have to eat crow.

- **egg on my face**

  Origin: probably alluding to performers being pelted with eggs for a bad performance.

  Idiomatic Meaning: embarrassment

  I got every answer on the quiz wrong. I sure had egg on my face.

- **every dog has its day**

  Origin: refers to the star Sirius—the "dog star"—and the consequences associated with its annual rising

  Idiomatic Meaning: everybody gets his or her chance to do something eventually

  Tyrese is never picked first in kickball, but I told him not to worry. Every dog has its day.

- **fair-weather friends**

  Idiomatic Meaning: friends who only associate with you when things are going well and disappear when times are tough.

  By not coming to see me in the hospital, Chris proved himself to be a fair-weather friend.

- **fall on deaf ears**

  Idiomatic Meaning: said of something, often advice, that is ignored or not listened to

  My mom kept telling me to clean my room, but her words were falling on deaf ears.

- **fifty-fifty**

  Idiomatic Meaning: equal

  I hope it doesn't rain for the field trip, but the chances are probably fifty-fifty.

- **flat broke**

  Idiomatic Meaning: having no money

  I would love to go to the show, but I'm flat broke. Maybe next time!

- **flea market**

  Origin: from a Paris, France, market where used goods were sold and presumed to carry vermin

  Idiomatic Meaning: any market, often outside, where large groups of people buy, sell, and swap used goods

  I usually don't wear sneakers, but these were so cheap at the flea market, I couldn't resist.

- **forty winks**

  Origin: To not get a wink of sleep is to not sleep at all; forty was once the all-purpose number to describe a lot of something.

  Idiomatic Meaning: a short nap

  If you and I are going to the late movie, I'm going to catch forty winks now.

- **get off the bench**

  Origin: from baseball, a game in which players who aren't playing sit on a bench

  Idiomatic Meaning: join in with others to get something done

  If Joey wants the extra credit for this assignment, he's going to have to get off the bench and help out.

- **get the ball rolling**

  Idiomatic Meaning: start something

  At first the party was a dud, but then we put on some music, and that got the ball rolling.

- **get one's goat**

  Origin: from the idea that goats are stubborn or cranky animals

  Idiomatic Meaning: annoy someone or to be annoyed

  My brother always insults how I am dressed, which really gets my goat.

- **get on one's nerves**

  Idiomatic Meaning: Annoy

  I was trying to watch TV, and my little brother's crying was really getting on my nerves.

- **give a run for one's money**

  Origin: from horseracing

  Idiomatic Meaning: compete on an equal, or almost equal, footing

  I've never beaten Amy in the chili cook-off before, but this year I'm going to give her a run for her money.

- **give it one's best shot**

  Idiomatic Meaning: try as hard as one can

  I've never done math problems as hard as these, but I'll give it my best shot.

- **(my) goose is cooked**

  Idiomatic Meaning: to be in trouble or difficulty

  I didn't study for my Spanish test and now my goose is cooked. I'll probably fail the test.

- **green around the gills**

  Origin: refers to the green pallor of skin when someone is ill

Idiomatic Meaning: looking unwell

Andrew looked green around the gills after that long boat ride.

- **green-eyed monster**

  Origin: This phrase was first used in the early 1600s by William Shakespeare in *The Merchant of Venice.*

  Idiomatic Meaning: jealousy

  Jenny had a bit of the green-eyed monster when I got picked for chorus and she didn't.

- **gut reaction**

  Idiomatic Meaning: an intuitive feeling

  Since it was late at night, my gut reaction was that walking home wasn't a smart idea.

- **half-baked**

  Origin: refers to a cake not being cooked all the way to the middle

  Idiomatic Meaning: not completely thought through

  A twenty-mile hike sounded good at first, but when we took into account the harsh weather and all the supplies we'd need, we realized it was a pretty half-baked idea.

- **have a cow**

  Origin: 1950s phrase that humorously reflects on what it would be like if a person actually gave birth to a full-grown cow

  Idiomatic Meaning: get very angry or upset about something

  My brother is going to have a cow when he sees that I broke his skateboard.

- **hold your horses**

  Origin: Pulling on the reins of a horse and holding them will make the horse stand still.

  Idiomatic Meaning: be patient or wait for something

  Hold your horses, I'm not ready to leave yet.

- **icing on the cake**

  Origin: Of course, icing makes an already delicious cake even tastier.

  Idiomatic Meaning: something that makes a good situation even better

  The fact that the dress I loved was also on sale was icing on the cake.

- **in a nutshell**

  Origin: Since nutshells are small, only something tiny could fit inside.

  Idiomatic Meaning: briefly, in a few words

  My teacher called me to her desk and told me, in a nutshell, how to improve my grades.

- **in for rough weather**

  Idiomatic Meaning: about to get difficult

  The man's company had been losing money, and he was worried that they were in for rough weather for the rest of the year.

- **in the ballpark**

  Idiomatic Meaning: in the generally right area (literally or conceptually)

  I didn't guess the exact number of jelly beans in the jar, but I was in the ballpark.

- **joined at the hip**

  Origin: This derives from Chang and Eng Bunker, conjoined twins made famous by PT Barnum in the late 1800s. The Bunker twins were not actually joined at the hip, but rather the chest.

  Idiomatic Meaning: inseparable

  After my best friend got home from sleep-away camp, we were joined at the hip for the rest of the summer.

- **keep your shirt on**

  Origin: Because clothes were once so expensive, men would remove their shirts before fighting, so as not to ruin them.

  Idiomatic Meaning: avoid losing one's temper; to remain calm

  Keep your shirt on. There's no reason to get so angry at Anthony.

- **learn by heart**

  Idiomatic Meaning: to memorize

  I had to learn my lines by heart for the school play.

- **leaves a bad taste in my mouth**

  Origin: based on the experience of eating bitter, unpleasant, or distasteful food

  Idiomatic Meaning: leaves a lingering bad feeling

  My fight with Claudia left a bad taste in mouth. I want to apologize.

- **look like something the cat dragged in**

  Origin: Cats kill their prey before bringing it inside.

  Idiomatic Meaning: look worn out or beaten up

  After a long day working outside in the heat, I know I looked like something the cat dragged in.

- **made in the shade**

  Idiomatic Meaning: in a good position

  Once we bike over that last hill, we'll have it made in the shade.

- **made of money**

  Idiomatic Meaning: possessing an endless supply of money, often said in the negative

  When I asked my mom for an expensive pair of jeans, she said, "Do you think I'm made of money?"

- **make one's blood run cold**

  Idiomatic Meaning: shock or horrify someone

  It made my blood run cold to hear about that car crash.

- **make the grade**

  Idiomatic Meaning: do well enough, succeed

  When it comes to salsa dancing, I really don't make the grade.

- **make a mountain out of a molehill**

  Origin: Mountains are big; molehills are small.

  Idiomatic Meaning: make something insignificant seem large or important

  My dad made a mountain out of a molehill just because I hadn't cleaned my room all week.

- **make one's skin crawl**

  Origin: refers to the feeling of insects crawling on your skin

  Idiomatic Meaning: frighten a person so much that he or she gets goose bumps

  I'm terrified of spiders—they make my skin crawl.

- **(a) million to one**

  Idiomatic Meaning: improbable; unlikely

  Our chances at getting to go to Disneyworld are a million to one.

- **no sweat**

  Origin: If you are taking it easy, you are not sweating.

  Idiomatic Meaning: without difficulty; not problematic; easy

  Passing the math test was no sweat because I had studied all weekend.

- **none of your beeswax**

  Origin: This comes from the days when smallpox was a common disease. Women would fill the pockmarks on their faces with beeswax to hide them. If the weather was warm, the wax would melt but it was considered ill form to tell a woman that her makeup was running.

  Idiomatic Meaning: none of your business

  I wanted to know what my sisters were fighting about but they told me it was none of my beeswax.

- **nose to the grindstone**

  Origin: A grindstone is used by blacksmiths to sharpen metal tools. When working, a blacksmith would have to bend forward over the stone to see his work.

  Idiomatic Meaning: to continually work diligently at something

  I had to keep my nose to the grindstone in order to learn how to play piano.

- **not my cup of tea**

  Idiomatic Meaning: something you don't like or enjoy

  I tried horseback riding last week, and discovered that it's not my cup of tea.

- **nuttier than a fruitcake**

  Origin: "Nuts" is a common term for crazy. Fruitcakes are commonly filled with nuts, thereby implying that someone "nuttier than a fruitcake" is extremely crazy.

  Idiomatic Meaning: crazy; usually said in jest

  My sister's favorite lunch is an olive and peanut butter sandwich. She's nuttier than a fruitcake!

- **old school**

  Origin: refers to an old-fashioned method of learning

  Idiomatic Meaning: done in a way that is outdated or old-fashioned

  I like all the new dances, but Jeannie dances old school.

- **on a silver platter**

  Idiomatic Meaning: effortlessly

  My brother has it so easy—everything is handed to him on a silver platter.

- **once in a blue moon**

  Origin: Rarely—once every 32 months or so—two full moons appear in the same month. Years ago, a second full moon was believed to cause certain weather conditions that made the moon appear blue.

  Idiomatic Meaning: very rarely, occasionally

  I love candy, but I'm only allowed to eat it once in a blue moon.

- **out in left field**

  Origin: refers to the back left side of a baseball field

  Idiomatic Meaning: unusual or offbeat

  Most of the time my brother makes a lot of sense, but sometime his ideas are really out in left field.

- **par for the course**

  Origin: This refers to the number of shots expected to be taken at any given hole on a golf course.

  Idiomatic Meaning: normal or expected in a situation

  It's par for the course that my sister got to stay up late while I had to go to bed at 9:30.

- **(a) penny for your thoughts**

  Origin: This dates back to the 1500s, when a penny was worth a lot more than it is now. Offering someone a penny meant you really wanted to know what they were thinking.

  Idiomatic Meaning: A phrase said in order to find out what someone else is thinking

  Hannah looked worried about something, so Kelly said, "A penny for your thoughts."

- **(a) piece of cake**

  Origin: This dates to the mid-19th century when, in slavery states, slaves or free descendents would walk in a line around a cake at a social gathering or party. The most graceful would be awarded a cake as a prize. This is also where we get the term "cake walk" which also means something easy to accomplish.

  Idiomatic Meaning: something that is easy to do

  I thought that painting my bedroom would be hard, but with help from my friends it was a piece of cake.

- **(a) pretty penny**

  Idiomatic Meaning: a lot of money

  My parents paid a pretty penny to fly us all out to visit my grandparents.

- **pull a rabbit out of a hat**

  Origin: This refers to a magician making rabbits or other objects appear from a hat.

  Idiomatic Meaning: to come up with an idea or object out of nowhere, as if by magic

  I didn't think John would do well on the math quiz but he kept coming up with answers as if he were pulling rabbits out of a hat.

- **put a bug in one's ear**

  Idiomatic Meaning: to give someone an idea about something that the person cannot then stop thinking about

  My sister put a bug in my ear about moving to Colorado, and now I can't stop thinking about it.

- **put one through one's paces**

  Origin: When buying a horse, you want to put it through its paces first—making sure that it can walk, trot, canter, etc. before you buy it.

  Idiomatic Meaning: to put someone through a rigorous test to show what they are capable of

  I thought I was a good speaker, but debate team really puts me through my paces!

- **put in one's two cents**

  Origin: Some believe that this originates with games like poker where players must pay an ante, or very small amount, to play. Others believe it comes from the 16th century British phrase "a penny for your thoughts."

  Idiomatic Meaning: to add your comments or opinions to a conversation

  When my parents were trying to decide where to take the family on vacation, I put in my two cents and suggested the beach.

- **put on one's thinking cap**

  Origin: This was originally termed a "considering cap" and used as a common phrase in the early 17th century.

  Idiomatic Meaning: to focus on and think hard about something

  I'll put on my thinking cap and see if I can figure out how to fix the broken faucet.

- **race against the clock**

  Idiomatic Meaning: hurry because time is running out

  We were racing against the clock to organize mom's surprise party before she got home.

- **raining cats and dogs**

  Origin: Many believe this phrase originated during the Black Death when many animals died in the streets. After a particularly hard rain, the bodies of many cats and dogs would often be awash in the streets.

  Idiomatic Meaning: rain very hard

  Our baseball game was cancelled because it has been raining cats and dogs all day.

- **round of golf**

  Origin: The word round is used in this phrase to mean an entire game

  Idiomatic Meaning: A game of golf

  In order to play a full round of golf today we had to get to the golf course very early.

- **see eye to eye**

  Idiomatic Meaning: agree

  When it comes to pizza, my dad and I see eye to eye. We both love pepperoni.

- **see red**

  Origin: In the sport of bull fighting, a red flag is used to tease the bulls, provoking their anger and making them charge at the bullfighter.

  Idiomatic Meaning: a state of rage; very angry

  Ordering a pizza for dinner after mom's been cooking all day will have her seeing red.

- **show your true colors**

  Origin: During sea battles, a ship would fly the flag of their enemy to get close to their opponent at sea without alarming them. Then, just before attacking, they would lower the false flag and raise their actual flag, thereby showing their true colors.

  Idiomatic Meaning: demonstrate what one is really like or what one is truly thinking

  Sometimes kids at school act really nice but then they show their true colors by doing something mean.

- **six of one, a half dozen of the other**

  Origin: based on the fact that half a dozen, or half of twelve, is equal to six

  Idiomatic Meaning: there is little difference between two options

  I think it's six of one, a half a dozen of the other whether we go out for pizza or have it delivered.

- **skin and bones**

  Idiomatic Meaning: to be very skinny

  After having stomach flu for two weeks, Carlos was skin and bones.

- **smell something fishy**

  Idiomatic Meaning: suspect that something is not right

  When my brother was being extra-nice to me, I smelled something fishy.

- **snowed under**

  Origin: This refers to a person being buried under work in the same way that objects are buried under snow after a large storm.

  Idiomatic Meaning: overworked or having too much to do

  With a book report due, three tests to study for, and baseball practice, I'm completely snowed under this week.

- **snug as a bug in a rug**

  Idiomatic Meaning: cozy and comfortable

  With my pj's on and a cup of hot chocolate in my hand, I was snug as a bug in a rug.

- **spill the beans**

  Idiomatic Meaning: tell a secret to someone who is not supposed to know about it

  I knew about my surprise party because my brother spilled the beans and told me it was being planned.

- **look one square in the face**

  Idiomatic Meaning: look at someone directly in the face

  I knew she wasn't lying to me because she looked me square in the face when she told me what had happened.

- **strike out**

  Origin: from baseball's rule that getting three strikes means a player is out

  Idiomatic Meaning: lose or fail

  I thought I would be good at chess, but every time I play, I seem to strike out.

- **take with a grain of salt**

  Origin: This phrase dates back to 1647 and refers to the discovery of a recipe for an antidote to poison in which one of the ingredients was a grain of salt. Thereafter threats involving the poison were to be taken "with a grain of salt" and therefore less seriously.

  Idiomatic Meaning: believe only a part of something or to look at something skeptically

  Mom said we could have cake for dessert if we behaved today, but since she never lets us have sweets I'm taking her comment with a grain of salt.

- **talk until you're blue in the face**

  Idiomatic Meaning: talk to the point of exhaustion, usually with the intention of convincing someone of something, and usually fruitlessly

  She talked until she was blue in the face but could not convince me to go mountain climbing with her.

- **talking in circles**

  Idiomatic Meaning: talk in a roundabout way

  I tried to understand what he was saying, but he was talking in circles and didn't make any sense.

- **tempest in a teapot**

  Idiomatic Meaning: a big fuss about something small or trivial

  We were all worried about Y2K, but it turned out it was just a tempest in a teapot.

- **that makes two of us**

  Idiomatic Meaning: phrase used to indicate that you and another person have something in common

  Anna didn't get enough sleep last night. That makes two of us.

- **the third degree**

  Origin: From the Freemason ritual of interrogating a member before bestowing the last (third) degree of membership, Master Mason.

  Idiomatic Meaning: cross examination

  When my sister and I came back from vacation a day late, the attendance clerk gave us the third degree.

- **three square meals**

  Origin: This dates back to the days of wooded sailing ships. So many adverse things made life on these ships difficult. If you made it through "three square meals" a day avoiding fires, scurvy, attacks, and so on, it was thought that you were doing pretty well.

  Idiomatic Meaning: eating three nutritious meals a day in order to remain in good health

  It is important to eat three square meals a day in order to be healthy.

- **tickled pink**

  Origin: Pink is often associated with being happy, and this expression dates all the way back to the 17th century when tickling was seen as a pleasurable light touch to the skin.

  Idiomatic Meaning: pleased by someone or something

  Grandma was tickled pink by your visit today.

- **travel in the same circles**

  Idiomatic Meaning: have lots of friends in common

  I don't really know Sophia well, but we travel in the same circles.

- **two bricks shy of a load**

  Origin: Making sure to have the right count of bricks is very important to a builder, as he might have to dangerously climb up or down to get more.

  Idiomatic Meaning: not very intelligent, usually said playfully

  Our dog Trixie thinks the garden hose is alive. I think she's two bricks shy of a load.

- **until the cows come home**

  Idiomatic Meaning: a long duration

  You can dig that hole until the cows come home, but you will never reach China.

- **up one's sleeve**

  Origin: This originates from magicians, who often hide things in their sleeves in order to make their tricks work.

  Idiomatic Meaning: secret or held in reserve, usually referring to some plan of action

  I don't know how we're going to win the basketball game, so I hope the coach has a plan up his sleeve.

- **wear one's heart on one's sleeve**

  Origin: During the Middle Ages, knights would often dedicate their performance in battle to a woman of the court—usually someone they were in love with. The knights would pin to one sleeve a scarf belonging to the woman, to let their feelings for her be known to all.

  Idiomatic Meaning: show your feelings

  After her grandpa died, Melissa had a hard time not wearing her heart on her sleeve. Everyone could see how sad she was.

- **(a) wolf in sheep's clothing**

  Origin: Both Aesop's fables and the Bible contain specific references to wolves in sheep's clothing.

  Idiomatic Meaning: someone who pretends to be a good person but really isn't

  I'm not sure if I should trust him. He seems like a wolf in sheep's clothing.

- **you bet your boots**

  Origin: Since people rarely had more than one pair of shoes or boots, they would only bet their boots if they were certain of the outcome.

  Idiomatic Meaning: definitely, with certainty

  You bet your boots I'm coming to see you in the play!